COUNTRY TOPICS FOR CRAFT PROJECTS

ITALY

Patricia Borlenghi and Rachel Wright
Illustrated by Teri Gower

FRANKLIN WATTS
New York ● Chicago ● London ● Toronto ● Sydney

This symbol appears on some
pages throughout this book. It
indicates that adult supervision
is advisable for that activity.

© Watts Books 1993

Franklin Watts
95 Madison Avenue
New York, NY 10016

10 9 8 7 6 5 4 3 2 1

Library of Congress Cataloging-in-Publication Data

Borlenghi, Patricia.
    Italy / by Patricia Borlenghi and Rachel Wright.
        p. cm — [Country Topics for Craft Projects]
    Includes index.
    Summary: Introduces the geographical, historical, and social
aspects of everyday life in Italy, examining the different regions,
trade, agriculture, and school and home life. Includes activities.
    ISBN 0-531-14264-7
    1. Italy—Social life and customs—20th century—Juvenile
literature. [1. Italy.] I. Wright, Rachel. II. Title. III. Series.
DG451.B68 1993
945.092—dc20   93-14702
                                                  CIP   AC

Editor: Hazel Poole
Consultant: Fabiana Ramella
Designer: Sally Boothroyd
Photography: Peter Millard
Artwork: John Shackell
Picture Research: Ambreen Husain, Juliet Duff

Printed in the United Kingdom

Contents

Introducing Italy

Benvenuti in Italia! Welcome to Italy! Before you start to explore, here are a few useful facts about the country.

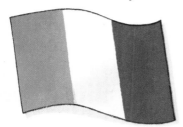

FLYING THE FLAG

The Italian flag, *la bandiera tricolore,* was first used in 1797. It has green, white, and red stripes and is similar to the French flag, but with a green stripe instead of blue. Green symbolizes nature and man's natural rights - equality and liberty.

ITALY IN THE WORLD

Italy lies in Southern Europe and is a peninsula surrounded by sea. It covers 116,303 square miles (301,245 sq km) and looks like a high-heeled boot with the island of Sicily at its toe. Italy borders France, Switzerland, Austria, and Slovenia.

Officially known as *la Repubblica Italiana*, Italy was one of the six founder members of the European Economic Community (EEC). It is one of the seven richest industrial countries in the world. The capital city is Rome - "the eternal city." The current population is over 57 million.

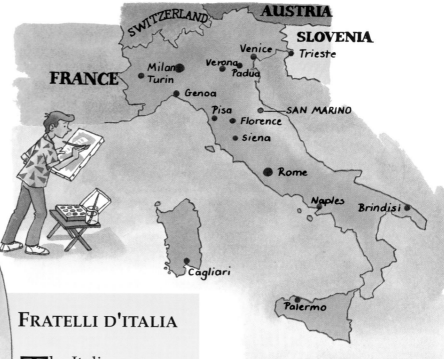

FRATELLI D'ITALIA

The Italian national anthem is *Fratelli d'Italia*, composed in 1847 by Goffredo Mameli, a patriot and poet. It became the national anthem in 1946.

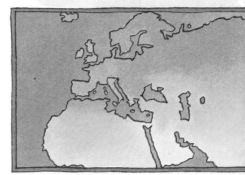

MONEY AND STAMPS

The currency is called the lira (plural = lire). It is written as LIT. The different coins are 50, 100, 200, and 500 lire. The woman's head on the coins symbolizes the republic. Notes are issued in 1000, 2000, 5000, 10,000, 50,000, and 100,000 lire denominations.

Stamps over 1000 lire also show the woman's head.

To make a public telephone call, you need a 200 lire coin or a "gettone" which equals 200 lire. You often get these in your change.

GOVERNMENT

The Head of State is the president, who is elected every seven years, but the prime minister runs the country. The parliament is made up of the Chamber of Deputies and the Senate, whose members are elected every five years. However, Italy's politics are beset by corruption and financial scandals.

CAR REGISTRATION

Italian car numbers are fun to identify. You can tell which city or town the car is from by looking at the license plate. For example, cars from Milan have MI on their license plate. The only place where the whole name is used is ROMA, for Rome.

THE MAFIA

The Mafia is a criminal organization from Sicily, made up of about 100 "families." The *Mafiosi* (Mafia members) control international drug-dealing and demand protection money from Italian businesses. They kidnap rich people and bribe politicians. In recent times, many important figures have been killed by them, but some members of the Mafia are now being caught and imprisoned.

Say it in Italian
la bandiera - flag
il francobollo - stamp
i soldi - money
l'Italia - Italy
gli italiani - the Italians
la carta - map

Around Italy

Italy is divided into 20 regions and 94 provinces. A lot of the land is hilly and some of the mountains are volcanic. The Alps stretch along the north and on the east they become known as the Dolomites. The Apennines run down the middle of the country and are known as the "backbone" of Italy.

Italy's regions are divided into provinces and municipalities called *comuni*. Each of these has an elected council. The regions must abide by the laws of the national government but they are allowed to make local laws.

San Marino is a tiny independent republic in its own right and has its own flag. It is one of the oldest states in Europe.

Vatican City is also a separate state occupying only 17 square miles (0.44 sq km). It has its own flag, currency, and stamps and there are some areas that can only be entered with special permission. The Pope lives in Vatican City.

DIALECTS

Italian is the official language. It is based on the Florentine dialect (from Florence). German and French are also spoken around the Italian borders. Each region has its own dialect, but there are many more variations. These have been influenced by French, German, Greek, Spanish, Arabic, and Celtic words. Sicilian is spoken in Sicily and Sardinians have their own dialect called "Sardo."

CLIMATE

In Northern Italy, winters are cold and wet but the summers are hot and dry. This is a continental climate. In the south, winters are mild, springs are sunny and summers are very hot and dry. This is a Mediterranean climate. In the winter, there is snow in the mountains, even in the south of Italy. The peaks of the Alps are always covered in snow, both in winter and summer.

Average temperatures		
Place	**January**	**July**
Milan	41°F	84°F
Rome	52°F	86°F
Naples	53°F	84°F

ARCHITECTURE

Italy contains a wonderful variety of architecture. In Roman times, town planning was very sophisticated. The Romans invented concrete and were the first to use the arched vault. They continued the Greek tradition of mosaics by pressing tiny bits of stone into wet plaster. The Romans used uniform shapes and matching numbers of arches and columns. They had a great influence on Italian artists of the Renaissance.

Today lots of monuments are crumbling, but most of the old city centers are preserved as they were many years ago.

POMPEII

Pompeii was a Roman town near Naples. In A.D. 79 it was buried by lava and ash from Mount Vesuvius, a volcano near Naples. You can still visit the ruins and see what Roman houses, streets, and shops used to look like.

THE COLISEUM

The Coliseum in Rome was used by the ancient Romans as an arena for sports and entertainment.

VOLCANOES

Italy is unique as it has two very famous and active volcanoes. The highest volcano in Europe is Mount Etna in Sicily at 10,902 feet (3,343 m) high. It still erupts today.

The Lipari (or Aeolian) islands include the volcano on Stromboli, which is still active. The beaches are full of black sand and pumice stone. Many islanders are scared of the volcano and call it "he."

7

The leaning Tower of Pisa

This is one of Italy's most famous landmarks. It is the bell tower of Pisa cathedral, and it is leaning so badly that it is now closed to the public and the bells have stopped ringing.

Venice

The city of Venice is built on 118 small islands, joined together by 100 canals. There are nearly 400 bridges crossing the canals. St. Mark's Square and St. Mark's Church are famous landmarks of this city.

La Basilica di san pietro

The Basilica, in Vatican City, Rome, is built on the spot where St. Peter was buried. This is the world's largest church and is very ornate.

Florence

Florence is a beautiful city situated on both sides of the Arno River. Cars are not allowed in many parts of the city. The *Duomo di Santa Maria del Fiore* is a main feature of this city.

Across the Arno is the famous *Ponte Vecchio* (Old Bridge) which houses lots of jewelry stores selling fine gold and silver.

Say it in Italian
l'estate - summer
la primavera - spring
l'autunno - autumn
il tempo - weather
il sole - sun
la pioggia - rain
la montagna - mountain

Mini Mosaics

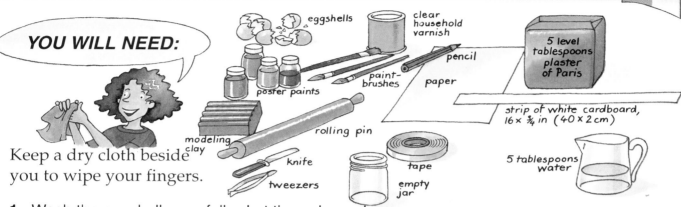

YOU WILL NEED:

eggshells

clear household varnish

pencil

paint-brushes

paper

poster paints

5 level tablespoons plaster of Paris

modeling clay

rolling pin

strip of white cardboard, 16 × ¾ in (40 × 2 cm)

knife

tweezers

tape

empty jar

5 tablespoons water

Keep a dry cloth beside you to wipe your fingers.

1. Wash the eggshells carefully. Let them dry and paint them. When the paint is dry, add a coat of varnish.

2. Roll out some clay about $^1/_4$ in ($^1/_2$ cm) thick.

3. Fold the cardboard into four and tape the ends together to make a square.

4. Press the cardboard square firmly into the clay.

5. Draw a simple design for your mosaic.

6. Break the eggshells into pieces. Try not to make the pieces too small!

7. Put the plaster of Paris and water into the jar and stir well with the knife.

8. Pour the plaster into the cardboard square. Using your design as a guide, carefully lay pieces of eggshell into the wet plaster. (Plaster of Paris dries quickly, so you will need to work fast.) As the plaster hardens, gently press the eggshells into place with the tip of the tweezers. (If a piece of eggshell lands upside down, turn it over with the tweezers.)

9. When the plaster of Paris is nearly dry, peel away the cardboard. When it is completely dry, remove the clay carefully.

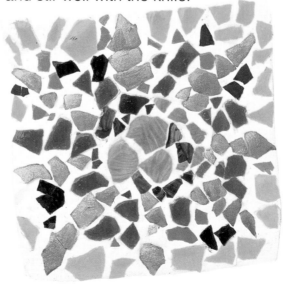

Shopping and Eating

Italy produces 20 percent of the world's wine, and there are vineyards in almost every region.

The Po Valley is the most important agricultural area in Italy, but there are small farms all over the country. Fruits such as oranges and lemons, peaches, apricots, plums, and tomatoes are grown. Other important crops are wheat, corn, olives, rice, sugar beet, tobacco, potatoes, artichokes, garlic, onions, cauliflowers, beans, and flowers. Cattle, sheep, goats, and pigs are reared on farms throughout the country, and fishing is widespread along the Italian coast.

Cheese is a major product of Italy. One of the most well-known is Parmesan cheese from Parma. Others include Mozzarella, made from buffalo milk, Bel Paese, Certosa, Fontina, and Mascarpone which is a cream cheese.

SHOPPING

There are now many supermarkets in Italy and also a few hypermarkets. However, many Italians like to buy fresh food daily, either from markets or small specialty stores.

Stores are usually open daily (except on Sundays) from 8:30 a.m. to 12:30 p.m. and 3:30 p.m. to 7:30 p.m. Banks in Italy are closed on Saturdays. They close one afternoon a week, but this varies regionally.

Shopping list

il pane - bread
il latte - milk
il formaggio - cheese
le uova - eggs
il tè - tea
le frutta - fruit
le verdure - vegetables
il pollo - chicken
il pesce - fish
il gelato - ice cream

Say it in Italian

il *supermercato* - supermarket
il *mercato* - market
il *panificio* - bakery
la *pasticceria* - pastry shop
la *macelleria* - butcher's shop
alimentari - grocer's shop
la *gelateria* - ice cream shop
la *farmacia* - drugstore
l'*ufficio postale* - post office
lil *banco* - bank

In Italy there are regional differences in cooking, but there is usually a standard menu wherever you go.

Because Italy is almost an island, fish is a very important part of the menu. Sardines get their name from Sardinia, famous for its fish soup.

Italians eat a lot of fresh fruit, but on feast days they will prepare special desserts. Such a dessert is *Tiramisù* (pick-me-up) which is made from layers of lady fingers dipped in black coffee, marsala, and mascarpone mixed with sugar. The top layer is sprinkled with chocolate powder. It is delicious.

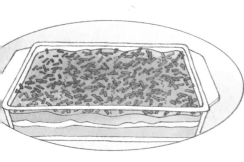

EATING OUT

Italians love eating out, especially with their families. They often go to restaurants for Sunday lunch. *Trattorie* are smaller restaurants but a good value, and *Tavole Calde* are inexpensive and serve hot food. *Rosticcerrie* serve take-out roasted meats and poultry. Street vendors sell everything from nuts and watermelons to pasta dishes.

Bars in Italy serve all kinds of drinks and sometimes brioche or croissants, panini (rolls), tramezzini (sandwiches), or tostati (toasted bread). They are open all day. Pizzerie (pizza parlors) are found all over Italy either for eating in or for take-out food.

PASTA

There are many varieties of pasta including spaghetti, tagliatelle, ravioli, penne, farfalle, ruote, paglia e fieno, vermicelli, tortelloni (big), and tortellini (small). Pasta is said to have been eaten in Etruscan times. It is usually served with a sauce or on its own with butter or olive oil, garlic and herbs.

MENU

Antipasto - hors d'oeuvres (usually includes a selection of cold meats including salami, coppa, bresaola, prosciutto, mortadella, or vegetable/fish salads)

Lasagne al forno - baked lasagne

Spaghetti alla Bolognese - spaghetti with meat sauce, from Bologna

Calamari - squid

Petti di Pollo - chicken breasts

Parmigiana di Melanzane - baked eggplant

Zabaglione - whipped egg, sugar, and wine dessert

Ice cream is another great Italian invention, and there are hundreds of different varieties.

A Passion for Pizza

Pizza, as we know it, was invented in Naples during the 1700s. Sold from street stalls, it soon became popular with the Neapolitans and before long, *pizzerie* were set up in the city. News of this tasty tomato-topped dish spread quickly, and when Italy's Queen Margherita visited Naples in 1889, she insisted on trying a pizza for herself. Immediately three different pizzas were made for the Queen, one of which was topped with tomatoes, mozzarella cheese, and basil. This was clearly the Queen's favorite and so it was named *Pizza Margherita*, in her honor.

To make four medium-sized Margherita pizzas.

YOU WILL NEED:

cling wrap
sieve
cheese grater
small bowl
2 large mixing bowls
metal spatula
wooden spoon
baking trays
oven mitts
knife
cup of hot water
½ pint warm water
½ teaspoon salt
4 teaspoons dried basil
4 tablespoons tomato puree
1 package fresh yeast
1 lb bread flour
olive oil
½ teaspoon sugar
6 tablespoons chopped canned tomatoes
¼ teaspoon vitamin C powder *
8 oz mozzarella cheese

*Vitamin C powder, or ascorbic acid, can be bought from most health food stores.

1. Stir the yeast and sugar into the warm water until they have dissolved. Let the mixture stand for 10 minutes.

2. Add the vitamin C powder and stir again.

3. Tip the flour and salt into the mixing bowl. Add the yeast mixture and 3 tablespoons of olive oil. Mix everything together with the wooden spoon until you have a soft, springy ball of dough that leaves the sides of the bowl clean. If the dough is too sticky, add a little more flour. If it is too dry, add a little more oil.

4. Sprinkle some flour over your hands and work surface, and knead the dough with your hands.

5. Rub some oil around the inside of the second bowl. Put in the dough, cover it with cling wrap, and leave it in a warm place for 15 minutes. (If the dough hasn't nearly doubled in size after 15 minutes, leave it a little longer.)

6. Preheat the oven to 425°F/220°C. Lightly grease the baking trays with oil and, using oven mitts, put them in the oven.

7. When the dough has doubled in size, cut it into four. Dip your knife into the cup of hot water, to keep the dough from sticking to it.

8. Cover your work surface and hands with flour, and flatten and stretch each portion of dough into a circle, about 8 in (20 cm) across. Pinch the edges of the circle with your fingers. This will keep the tomato topping from dripping off as the dough

9. Drain the canned tomatoes well. Put them in the small bowl with the tomato puree and stir. Spread an equal amount of this mixture over each doughy base.

10. Grate the cheese and divide it between the four bases. Sprinkle a teaspoon of basil over each base and add a drop of olive oil.

11. Take the baking trays out of the oven. Transfer your pizzas to the trays and put them in the oven. Bake them for 15-20 minutes and serve at once.

What do the Italian flag and a Margherita pizza have in common?

Life in Italy

HOUSING

Most Italians live in apartments in cities or towns. Their homes are quite small, but usually have a *cantina* (cellar) for storing wine and other goods. People living in the suburbs generally own houses with gardens or backyards.

Northern Italy, with its crowded, polluted, traffic-filled cities enjoys a greater standard of living than the poorer, more agricultural southern region. The South is less advanced because of its lack of industry.

Italians often have second homes in the country areas where their families originally lived. They often spend weekends there.

GOING TO SCHOOL

Children must go to school between the ages of 6-14. They attend *la scuola elementare* (primary school) until they are eleven. There are two types of timetable - one for full-time school, five days a week, and one for six mornings and some afternoons only. After primary school, children attend *la scuola media inferiore* (junior secondary school) for three years. At the age of fourteen, children decide what subjects they wish to study at *la scuola media superiore* (senior secondary school). There are three kinds to choose from - *il liceo*, specializing in classics, arts, languages, or sciences; *la scuola tecnica*, technical school with courses in

commerce, industry, or agriculture; *l'istituto magistrale* for primary school teacher training qualification (although some go on to college). After five years, students take a national exam - *l'esame di stato* - in order to get into college. Italy has 59 universities in 36 cities.

RELIGION

Italy is predominantly a Roman Catholic country. Only one percent of the population are Jewish, Protestant, or Greek Orthodox. The Pope lives in Vatican City in Rome and is the head of the Roman Catholic Church. People travel from all over the world to visit the Vatican.

Children make their first Holy Communion at the age of 7-10. Girls wear long white dresses and veils and boys wear suits.

At the age of 9 - 14, they are confirmed by a bishop. They also wear special or smart clothes on this occasion.

WHAT PEOPLE DO

Today more people work in industry than in agriculture. Others are employed in the wine and fishing industries. There are many public service employees. In Italy, many forms are needed for even the simplest things - but it does keep people employed.

THE POLICE FORCE

In Italy there are many different types of police. The *vigili urbani* (traffic police) wear white uniforms with white helmets and gloves in the summer, navy blue uniforms in the winter. They form part of the municipal police. The *Carabinieri* (Italian army corps) wear gray-green uniforms in the summer and black in the winter. They deal with crime and demonstrations.

THE MEDIA

Italy has more than 70 national daily newspapers. One of the most popular is *Corriere della Sera*, published in Milan. There are many weekly women's magazines including *Grazia, Marie Claire,* and *Donna Moderna*. There are also news, topical, and gossip magazines.

Italians love to watch television and officially there are 13 channels to choose from. There are three state-controlled channels but there are also over 100 independent or pirate stations.

Emergency telephone numbers
police 113
carabinieri 112
fire 114
road assistance and tourist advice 116

Say it in Italian:
l'insegnante - teacher
il medico - doctor
la scuola - school
la chiesa - church
il giornale - newspaper
il lavoro - work
la casa - house

Industry and Technology

INDUSTRY

Italy is the fourth biggest steel producer in Europe. Milan and Turin are the biggest industrial centers in Italy. The country is not rich in natural resources but has deposits of iron ore, lead, zinc, aluminum, and mercury. Italy has some coal and oil but most raw materials are imported. The hydroelectric industry - water being converted into electricity - is a major industry in the areas around the Alps. Italy is very rich in marble, and many homes have marble floors. The most famous marble is found at the Carrara quarries in Tuscany.

Sculptures are modelled from marble cut from the Carrara quarries in Tuscany.

TECHNOLOGY

Steel is necessary for Italy's car industry. Several well-known makes of car, such as Fiat, Alfa Romeo, Lancia, Lamborghini, and Ferrari are made in Italy and exported all over the world.

Many household appliances, such as washing machines, dishwashers, and refrigerators are made in Italy by companies like Zanussi.

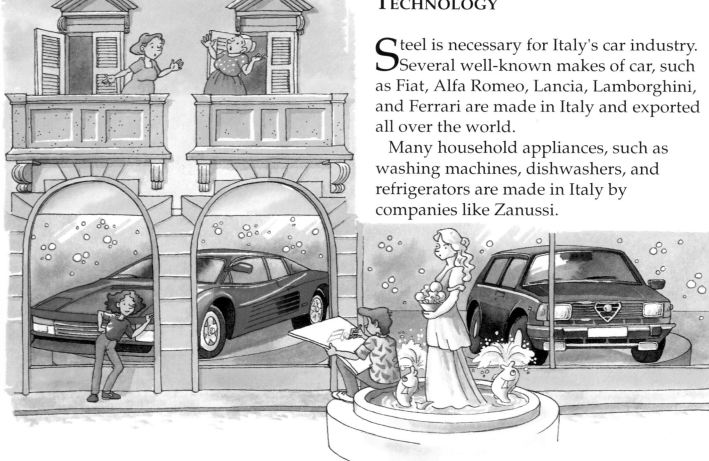

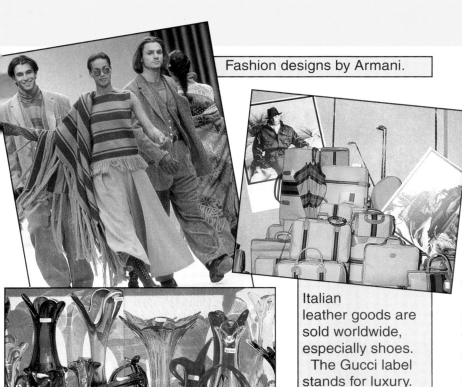

Fashion designs by Armani.

Italian leather goods are sold worldwide, especially shoes. The Gucci label stands for luxury.

Venetian glass is well-known for its ornamental designs.

FASHION AND DESIGN

Italians are renowned for design, both in clothing and home furnishing. The fashion and clothing industry is as important as tourism. Milan is famous for its *Collezioni* - the fashion collections. The greatest Italian fashion designers include Georgio Armani, Valentino, and Giovanni Versace. Italian design is very expensive and exclusive, but it is based on simple lines and elegance.

TRANSPORTATION

The public transportation system is very well run. Rail fares are cheap and there are several different types of train from the IC (InterCity) train to *locale* (a slower, local train stopping at every station).

Most cities and towns run cheap bus or tram services. The tickets are one price and can be bought from the *tabaccaio* or *edicola* (newsstand).

There is a huge highway system (*autostrade*) which is the third largest in the world.

Italy's airports are smaller than other airports, but they are very busy and *Alitalia*, Italy's national airline, carries over 7 million people worldwide. In the summer months, you can fly direct to most of Italy's major tourist resorts.

Say it in Italian:
la macchina - car
il treno - train
l'autobus - bus
l'aereo - airplane
il viaggio - journey
il metro - subway

17

Tourism, Sports and Leisure

The islands of Capri and Ischia, near Naples, are very picturesque.

Italy is so beautiful and rich in culture that tourism is its most important industry, with hundreds of thousands of people visiting the country each year. There are many seaside resorts, but some have become polluted and crowded, especially on the Adriatic coast. The beaches there are popular because they are long and sandy. On the Mediterranean, the Ligurian coast is rocky and sheltered. Further south, the beaches become less crowded.

Here are just a few of the tourist spots in Italy:

SICILY

Sicilia has been influenced by many cultures and Siracusa is the birthplace of Archimedes. There are many interesting Greek temples to visit.

THE MOUNTAINS

The Alps and the Dolomites are excellent for skiing. Popular resorts are Courmayeur, near Mont Blanc, and Cortina d'Ampezzo. Italians also ski in the Appenines on weekends.

THE LAKES

The lakes south of the Alps are popular for tourists and for windsurfers. The most famous of these lakes are Como, Maggiore, and Garda.

SPORTS AND LEISURE

Although Italians love skiing, tobogganing, and winter sports in general, the most popular sport is soccer. There are famous clubs such as Juventus, Inter, AC Milan, and Lazio.

Rugby and golf are becoming increasingly popular and Italian rugby has now reached world-class standard.

Bicycling is another national favorite with the *Giro d'Italia* held in June. Car racing fans watch the Grand Prix at Monza, near Milan, or at Imola near Bologna.

Italians love to play card games and although they use conventional playing cards, they have a different set of cards from Naples. These have suits of swords (spades), cups (hearts), money (diamonds), and sticks (clubs).

Say it in Italian:
il calcio - soccer
la squadra - team
la partita - game
nuotare - to swim
fare vela - to sail
fare una partita a carte - to play cards

19

The Arts

Italy has, over many centuries, created many masterpieces in all areas of the arts - painting, music, literature, and films. Italian museums are full of Etruscan art and pieces from the Magna Graecia period and there are many examples of early Christian art such as the beautiful mosaics in Ravenna *(left)*.

ART

Italy's wealth of art really began in the eleventh and twelfth centuries with the rise of Romanesque art and individual artists such as Nicola Pisano (1220-1278).

Giotto (di Bondone, 1266/7-1337), the greatest genius of the Italian Gothic period, came from Tuscany. He introduced fresco cycles - telling the story of a saint or prophet in the form of pictures. His greatest achievement is the St. Francis cycle at Basilica di St. Francesco in Assisi.

The Renaissance was Italy's most spectacular artistic period. Famous artists of that time include Sandro Botticelli (1445-1510), Fra Filippo Lippi (1406-1469), Titian (Tiziano Vecellio, 1488-1576), Raphael (Raffaello Sanzio 1483-1520), and Donatello (Donato de Betto di Bardi, 1386-1466) to name but a few.

LEONARDO DA VINCI (1452-1519)

Leonardo da Vinci painted many masterpieces such as the *Mona Lisa* and *The Last Supper*. His anatomical drawings and interest in science made him a true Renaissance figure. He invented many things including a flying machine.

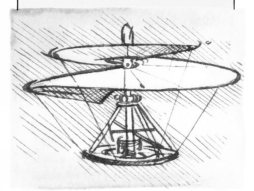

MICHELANGELO BUONARROTI (1475-1564)

Michelangelo painted the Sistine Chapel in Rome and also created the sculptures of David and the Pietà *(right)*, carved from Carrara marble.

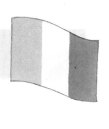

MUSIC

Music is another great Italian tradition. One of the most famous Italian composers is Antonio Vivaldi (1678-1741) who composed *The Four Seasons*.
Italy is the home of popular opera and some of the most famous operas in the world were composed by Italians.

GIUSEPPE VERDI (1813-1901)

Il Trovatore and *Rigoletto* (composed between 1851 and 1852) made Verdi famous in Italy. He later achieved world recognition with his later works such as *Aida* (1871), *Otello* (1887), and *Falstaff* (1893).

GIACOMO PUCCINI (1858-1924)

The works of Puccini include *La Bohème, Tosca, Madame Butterfly* and *Turandot*.

GIOACCHINO ROSSINI (1792-1868)

Rossini is famous for operas such as *The Barber of Seville* and *William Tell*.

Italy is also famous for its great singers including the tenor Enrico Caruso (1873-1921) and Luciano Pavarotti who made *Nessun Dorma* a great success during the Football World Cup of 1990.

LITERATURE

Famous Italian writers include the poet Dante Alighieri (1265-1321) who wrote *The Divine Comedy.* Other renowned medieval writers were Francesco Petrarch (1304-1374), Giovanni Boccaccio (1313-75) who wrote the *Decameron* - 100 witty stories - and Machiavelli, author of *The Prince* - a book about political theory. A famous author of today is Umberto Eco who wrote *The Name of the Rose*, a medieval whodunit.

THEATER

Italian theater flourished in the sixteenth century with the Commedia dell'Arte and the comic plays of the Venetian playwright Carlo Goldoni. The famous characters of the Commedia dell'Arte are *Pantalone, Dottore Graziano, Brighella,* and *Arlecchino* (Harlequin [*below*]). They usually wore masks and each character spoke his own dialect.

A recent successful movie from Italy has been *Cinema Paradiso* (1992).

MOVIES

Modern filmmaking is another great part of Italy's artistic heritage, with movie directors such as Roberto Rossellini , Federico Fellini, Franco Zeffirelli, and Bernardo Bertolucci.

Say it in Italian:
la musica - music
il artista - artist
la pittura- painting
il libro - book
il teatro - theater
il cine - film

Holidays and Festivals

Italy has 10 national holidays a year. Whenever one falls on a Thursday or a Tuesday, Italians usually take the Friday or Monday as holiday as well. On these national holidays, banks, public offices, most stores and some museums and galleries are closed.

Italians love festivals and local feast days are held in honor of each town's patron saint. There is usually a procession where a statue of the saint is carried around the town or village.

The traditional Pope's blessing is held every Easter Sunday in the Vatican, and in July the *Noiantri* (we others) festival is held in Trastevere, the old quarter of Rome. This is a street festival of music and fireworks by the Tiber river.

There are many festivals around August 15, and this is the time when Italians take their vacations. Stores can be closed for the whole month.

The week before Ash Wednesday is known as *Carnevale* (goodbye to meat) or Carnival. People all over Italy wear fancy dress and there are fairs and processions . The Carnival in Venice is very famous and everyone dresses up in masks and eighteenth century costume. There is a procession of gondolas along the Grand Canal and many masked balls are held.

In Florence on Easter Sunday morning, the *Scoppio del Carro* takes place in front of the cathedral. A highly decorated cart is filled with fireworks which are lit when a mechanical dove is freed from the altar of the cathedral. This festival commemorates the day on which knights returned to Florence after the First Crusade.

The *Palio* in Siena is a horse race held on July 2 and August 15 each year. People from different quarters dress in fifteenth century costume and form a procession to the main square. There is a display of flag-throwing and bareback horse riders from ten of the quarters race around the square. The winner gets a huge painted silk flag - the Palio.

The Palio, Siena.

The Palio, Siena.

Christmas celebrations start on December 24 with a big evening meal and Midnight Mass. Presents are exchanged both on Christmas Day and on January 6, the Epiphany. Tombola is a game played by many families during the Christmas period. It can be played by any number of players and a caller.

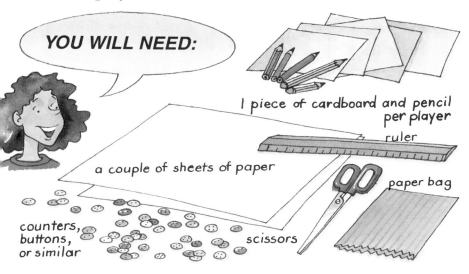

YOU WILL NEED:

1 piece of cardboard and pencil per player

ruler

a couple of sheets of paper

paper bag

counters, buttons, or similar

scissors

To make the game

1. Rule 20 small squares onto each piece of cardboard. Write a number from 1 - 50 in each square.

2. Draw 50 squares, the same size as the ones you have just drawn, onto a piece of paper. Number them from 1 - 50, cut them out, and put them in the paper bag.

To play the game

The caller picks the squares out of the bag, one at a time, and calls out the numbers. Players then cover any numbers that they have on their cards. The first player to cover a complete card calls out "Tombola" and is the winner.

In Naples on New Year's Day, fireworks are lit and people throw old things out of the windows. All the ships in the harbor sound their horns.

In the wine-producing areas, there is always a celebration at harvest time in the autumn. There are fairs and dancing when the new wine is tasted.

Say it in Italian:
le ferie - holidays
la festa - festival
il Natale - Christmas
la Pasqua - Easter
il compleanno - birthday
l'onomastico - saint's day

Mystery Masks

To disguise yourself for a Venetian Carnival ...

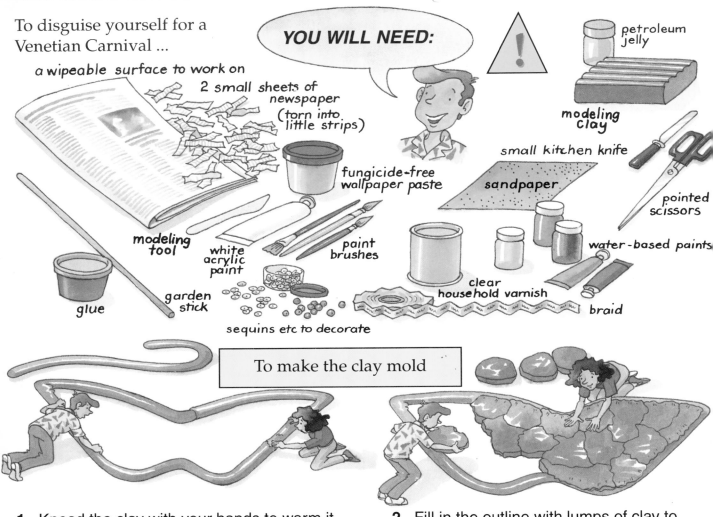

YOU WILL NEED:

a wipeable surface to work on

2 small sheets of newspaper (torn into little strips)

petroleum jelly

modeling clay

fungicide-free wallpaper paste

small kitchen knife

sandpaper

pointed scissors

modeling tool

white acrylic paint

paint brushes

clear household varnish

water-based paints

glue

garden stick

sequins etc to decorate

braid

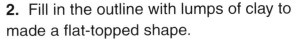

To make the clay mold

1. Knead the clay with your hands to warm it. Roll some of it into thick "sausages" and use these to form the outline of a half mask.

2. Fill in the outline with lumps of clay to made a flat-topped shape.

3. Hold the clay mold against your face and carefully mark the position of your eyes.

4. Cut holes for your eyes with the knife. Smooth the edges of these holes with the modeling tool.

5. Add small lumps of clay to make a nose. Blend the nose into the mold with the modeling tool.

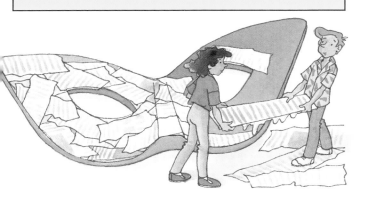

10. Once the acrylic paint has dried, you can paint your mask any color you like. To give your colors a shiny finish, add a coat of clear varnish once the paint has dried.

11. To decorate your mask, glue braid, sequins, or other trimmings onto the front of your mask.

6. Cover the surface of the clay mold with petroleum jelly. Dip some of the newspaper strips into the wallpaper paste and cover the mold with a layer of paper. Wait for the glued paper to dry and add another layer. Your mask will need about six layers in total.

12. Ask an adult to carefully pierce a small hole in the bottom rim of the mask. Paint the garden stick, push it through the hole, and glue it to the back of your mask.

7. When your mask is completely dry, ease it away from the mold.

8. Gently rub your mask with sandpaper to smooth it, and trim the edges with the scissors.

9. Paint your mask with a coat of white acrylic paint. This will help strengthen the papier mâché and leave you with a good surface for painting.

Italian History

Italy is an old country with a lot of history. Here are just a few key events and people.

THE ETRUSCANS

Nobody is sure where the Etruscans came from, but between 700 and 500 B.C., they ruled in Tuscany, north to the Po Valley, and south toward Naples. Their society was highly organized and evidence can be seen of their tombs, gold and metal ornaments, buildings, roads, canals, and sewers.

MAGNA GRAECIA

The Etruscans were influenced by the Greeks who, arriving in the eighth century B.C., set up colonies in Sicily, Naples, Paestum, and Taranto. The Greek mathematician, Pythagoras, invented his famous theory in Calabria.

ROME

According to legend, Rome was founded by Romulus in 753 B.C. Romulus and his twin brother Remus were abandoned by their mother and suckled by a she-wolf. This is Rome's symbol. Rome broke free from Etruscan rule in 509 B.C. and established a republic that lasted five centuries.

Julius Caesar ended the Republic by becoming a dictator. He was assassinated on the Ides of March (15th) 44 B.C. His adopted son, Augustus, established the Roman Empire in 30 B.C. The invasion by Attila the Hun and the sacking of Rome by the Goths and Vandals brought an end to the Roman Empire in Italy.

CHARLEMAGNE

In A.D. 800, Charlemagne had conquered Italy and was crowned by the Pope as emperor in Rome.

MARCO POLO

Marco Polo (1254-1324), from Venice, sailed to the Orient and brought back many treasures.

CITY STATES

Rivalry became stronger than ever in the twelfth century and Italy as a whole became impossible to rule. Independent communes became city-states. These included Venice, Genoa, Florence, and Milan, ruled by the *Visconti* family.

GALILEO GALILEI
(1564-1642)

Galileo was a great mathematician and inventor of the telescope. He was hounded by the church for saying that the earth was round and one of many planets in orbit around the sun.

VIVA VERDI!

In the nineteenth century, there was a great struggle for the unification of all the separate Italian states. It was led by Giuseppe Mazzini, Giuseppe Garibaldi, and Count Camillo di Cavour. Public meetings were banned and the opera house became one of the few places where large numbers of Italians could gather legally.

Verdi's operas were famous for their patriotic messages and as more patriots began to look to the king as a future leader of a united Italy, Verdi's name took on new significance. By shouting their approval of the composer, they could also send a coded message of defiance - V.E.R.D.I! - Vittorio Emanuele, Re D'Italia!

TIME BAND

9th c. b.c. Etruscans settle in Italy
8th c. b.c. Greeks in Sicily and the South
509 b.c. Roman Republic established
49-44 b.c. Julius Caesar rules as dictator
a.d. 79 Pompeii and Herculaneum are destroyed by the eruption of Vesuvius
800 Charlemagne crowned emperor in Rome
1860 Garibaldi's Expedition of a Thousand
1861 Kingdom of Italy formed
1870 Rome made capital of unified Italy
1915 Italy joins British, French, and Russians in World War I
1921 Italian Communist Party founded
1929 Lateran Treaty establishes a separate Vatican State
1936 Italy invades Abyssinia
1940 Italy joins Germany in World War II
1949 Italy becomes member of NATO
1958 Italy joins EEC

MUSSOLINI AND FASCISM

In the depression after World War I, Benito Mussolini (1883-1945) founded the Fascist party in 1921. He marched on Rome as leader *(Il Duce)* of the Fascists and formed a government in 1922. Mussolini supported Hitler in World War II. After the American liberation in 1943, he fell from power and was executed in 1945.

Say it in Italian:
la storia - history
il re - king
il soldato - soldier
il presidente - president
la politica - politics

29

Picture Pairs

Play Picture Pairs and see how many of the Italian words in this book you actually remember! The instructions given here are for two to four players, but as your Italian vocabulary increases, you might like to make more cards and include more players.

YOU WILL NEED:

OLD MAGAZINES
WRAPPING PAPER
METAL RULER
GLUE
SCISSORS
STIFF PAPER
THICK CARDBOARD
CUTTING BOARD
PAINTS OR CRAYONS
PENCIL
CRAFT KNIFE

To make the cards

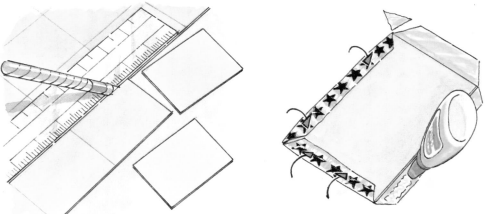

1. Draw 50 rectangles of the same size onto the cardboard and carefully cut them out using the craft knife.

2. Draw another 50 rectangles onto the wrapping paper and cut them out too. These rectangles should be about $3/4$ inch (2 cm) longer and wider than the cardboard ones.

3. Cut the the corners of the paper rectangles as shown and glue them onto your cards.

4. Draw 25 rectangles, slightly smaller than your cards onto the stiff paper and cut them out.

5. Choose 25 Italian words from this book and write them down with their English translations. (Keep this list beside you when you play the game.)

6. Look through the magazines and cut out any photographs that illustrate the words you have chosen. If you can't find suitable pictures, cut out some more rectangles from stiff paper and paint pictures of your words on them.

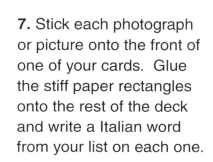

7. Stick each photograph or picture onto the front of one of your cards. Glue the stiff paper rectangles onto the rest of the deck and write a Italian word from your list on each one.

To play the game
The object of Picture Pairs is to collect pairs of cards made up of words and their matching picture.

Each player starts the game with seven cards. The rest of the deck is placed face-down on the table. If you have any pairs, put them on the table in front of you.

Then ask one of the other players if he/she has a card that you need to make a pair. If that player has the card requested, he/she must hand it over and you win the pair and take another turn. If he/she does not have the card, you take a card from the deck in the middle and the turn passes to the next person.

All word cards must be translated into English. If you cannot remember the translation of a word, look it up and miss your next turn.

The player who pairs all his/her cards first is the winner.

Index